Two Dark Thirty

Companion Workbook

Official

Marc Hill

smoky coast

Smoky Coast Press

Two Dark Thirty Official Companion Workbook

Copyright © 2022 by Marc Hill

Printed in the United States of America. For Smoky Coast Press. Wausau, Wisconsin 54401.

www.twodarkthirty.com

First Edition 2022

ISBN 979-8-9869893-3-4 (Paperback)

Cover designed by author

Pictures all courtesy of the author

All rights reserved.

No portion of this book may be copied or distributed in any form without written permission from the publisher or author, except as permitted by U.S. copyright law.

Puzzles made at puzzle-maker.com, puzzl.org, and mazepuzzlemaker.com

10 9 8 7 6 5 4 3 2 1

CONTENTS

FOREWORD

Two Dark Thirty will inspire you to grow your teaching and learning in emergency services. This companion workbook will enhance and boost your understanding and education while reading the main text. The workbook will guide you through each captivating chapter. The questions will challenge you to apply, adapt, and develop your new knowledge. Using this workbook, as a true companion to your reading, will greatly improve your content mastery. Even more resources and materials are located at twodarkthirty.com and if you haven't picked up your copy of the main text get over to Amazon.com and buy it today!

Good luck and stay safe.

Marc

INTRODUCTION

The following is a list of some questions that may be used to create discussion and further exploration of the topics covered in the chapters of the book. These are only examples, and I tried my best to make them discussion questions. I encourage you to create your own list and to foster more learning by evaluating my own questions and the book itself. I hope that you have enjoyed this book and have come away with a new understanding of what it may take to be a great teacher. Remember that in this profession, we all need to be open and honest. Don't let your ego stop you from learning. Education is a lifelong journey and one that I hope never ends for you. There is always something new to know, understand, and investigate. Be curious and ask questions. Help those who are looking for support and offer it to those who seem to be struggling. This is a service career. No other job or skill can be done without a teacher. Whether you are in a business or whether you are in the military, we all need great teachers. We all need to have someone show us the ropes and learn. Be the kind of teacher you would want to have.

Attitudes are contagious. Have one worth catching!

CHAPTER ONE

WHERE DO I BEGIN?

Mr. Hill's Notes:

- Start by being a storyteller.

- Be engaging and use your senses to teach.

- Involve your students in learning. Have a plan to captivate your students.

- Consider bringing in a guest speaker!

- Mindset and attitude are everything.

- Be positive!

1. What are the five parts that make a great story?

1.

2.

3.

4.

5.

2. Brainstorm some story ideas you could use for a lesson.

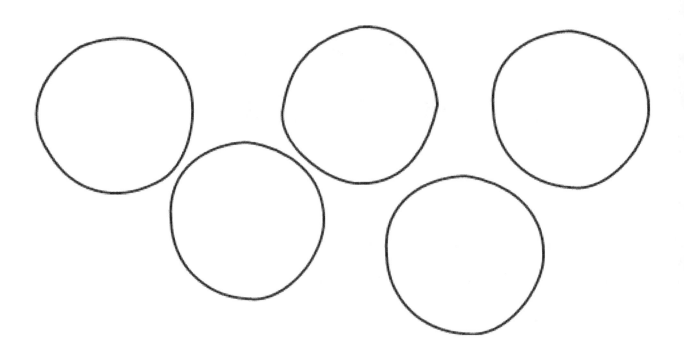

3. How do you plan on using those storytelling ideas in your lesson?

4. Outside of your own stories where else can you find story ideas?

5. Why is it important to engage a student in the learning process?

6. What was your favorite way that a teacher sought your engagement in class or in what ways do you wish a teacher had engaged you?

7. How does your attitude affect other people's impressions?

7 Self-doubt is normal and natural. Explain how you plan to keep getting better at your current position.

8. Think about a lesson you do not enjoy. Now break that lesson into parts you could find a guest speaker. List them below.

"If you find something very difficult to achieve yourself, don't imagine it impossible—for anything possible and proper for another person can be achieved as easily by you."
— Roman Emperor Marcus Aurelius

Chapter One Notes:

_____

_____

_____

_____

_____

_____

_____

_____

_____

_____

_____

_____

_____

_____

_____

_____

_____

_____

Where do I Begin
Word Search

```
S  I  M  P  O  S  T  E  R  E  D  G  D  Z  Y  L  G
T  E  C  N  A  C  I  F  I  N  G  I  S  R  M  R  M
O  N  E  V  I  T  I  S  O  P  A  A  A  D  K  Z  T
R  G  O  J  L  T  C  S  G  T  H  T  G  X  T  Q  L
Y  E  Y  I  M  A  N  O  T  X  I  C  N  N  M  X  D
T  M  C  D  T  A  R  E  N  L  B  I  A  M  E  N  R
E  Y  Y  N  K  A  N  O  I  T  A  T  C  E  P  X  E
L  C  C  E  A  T  N  M  G  T  A  R  R  E  R  A  L
L  A  L  N  I  L  A  I  R  N  H  G  V  A  T  K  T
I  P  E  O  E  R  U  E  G  C  I  I  I  T  E  P  X
N  T  N  V  A  G  T  B  T  A  T  K  I  O  A  H  J
G  I  O  P  E  N  R  A  M  A  M  T  A  R  U  H  T
D  V  S  Y  E  I  P  E  E  A  U  I  A  E  U  S  G
D  A  S  B  D  S  L  R  M  D  Z  B  T  M  P  R  T
N  T  E  M  I  D  C  E  E  E  L  L  A  T  M  S  Y
V  E  L  D  M  G  D  D  B  E  Y  N  M  Q  J  L  J
```

AMBULANCE	STORYTELLING	ATTENTION	SIGNIFICANCE	PARAMILITARY
EMERGENCY	DISPATCH	CONTAGIOUS	PARABLE	ENGAGE
HUMAN	HEART	IMAGINATION	CREATIVE	CAPTIVATE
ENTERTAIN	LESSON	REACH	ATTITUDE	EXPECTATION
IMPOSTER	BELIEVE	POSITIVE	SPEAKING	SNAKE

Chapter Two
The Fundamentals of Education

Mr. Hills Notes:

- The curriculum will help you know where to go.

- Have multiple types of learning activities ready.

- Review and repeat the information.

- Learning with your students is okay!

- Be open and ready to answer questions.

- Encourage others to participate and teach.

- Have realistic expectations of your students.

- Use evaluation to improve your class and yourself.

1. Give a definition of curriculum and then explain it in your own words.

2. How can you use the curriculum for your course?

3. Why are lesson plans important?

4. What does Maslow's Hierarchy of needs tell us about our students?

5. Explain three ways you can use Maslow's Needs in your class.

1.

2.

3.

6. How can you combine Bloom's Taxonomy and Gardner's Multiple Intelligences?

7. KISS is a great way to plan for a lesson. In what ways can you incorporate KISS in your lesson planning?

8. SMART goals are a great tool for students. Define your own SMART goal below.

Specific (What goals will be met? What steps are you going to take?):

Measurable (What data will be used to gauge success? What amount?):

Achievable (Is the target attainable? Do you own the tools and resources expected?):

Relevant (How does the goal fit in with bigger objectives? Why is the outcome meaningful?):

Time-bound (What is the planned timeline for achieving the goals?):

9. CRM is also referred to as the "pit crew" mindset. How can you use this team mentality in your class?

10. OODA Loop is a great situational awareness construct. Create an illustration of the process below.

11. What does a student evaluation tell you?

12. Describe three different types of evaluations will you use in your course and how they relate to Bloom's Taxonomy.

13. What was your favorite way a teacher evaluated you?

14. Explain how you can use the "Sandwich Method" in giving criticism to a student.

"If you're not making mistakes, then you're not doing anything.
I'm positive that a doer makes mistakes."
—John Wooden

Chapter Two Notes:

Fundamentals of Education
Crossword

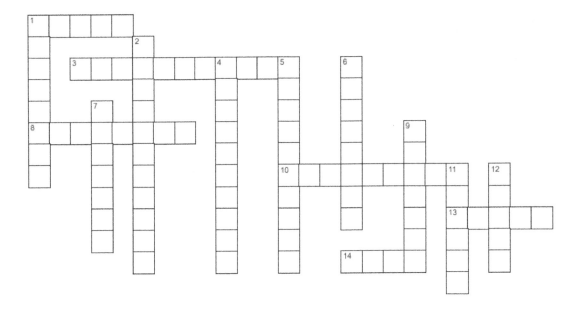

ACROSS

1 Taxonomy.

3 Physical hands-on learning.

8 Boyd's Cycle.

10 Best when used as a sandwich.

13 Specific, measurable, achievable, relevant, time-bound.

14 Keep it super simple.

DOWN

1 Dr. Wong's system to begin class.

2 types of learning styles the instructor will incorporate.

4 how the teacher plans to test the student's knowledge.

5 the courses offered by an educational institution.

6 Book learning.

7 Frames of Mind.

9 Short, simple, and top-of-head knowledge.

11 A Theory of Human Motivation.

12 Crew Resource Management.

CHAPTER THREE
HOW TO BE A SUCCESSFUL TEACHER

Mr. Hill's Notes:

- Clearly communicate the rules.

- Manage your classroom effectively with flexibility and firmness.

- Empathy and compassion have their place.

- Be prepared for class.

- Don't reinvent the wheel. Start filling your toolbox.

- Celebrate the successes and the failures.

- Keep motivating students' success.

- Learn from your mistakes.

1. What is a formal classroom?

2. What are the three types of teaching styles?

1.

2.

3.

3. Participation is a key to success in teaching. Brainstorm how do you plan to participate in the lesson with your students.

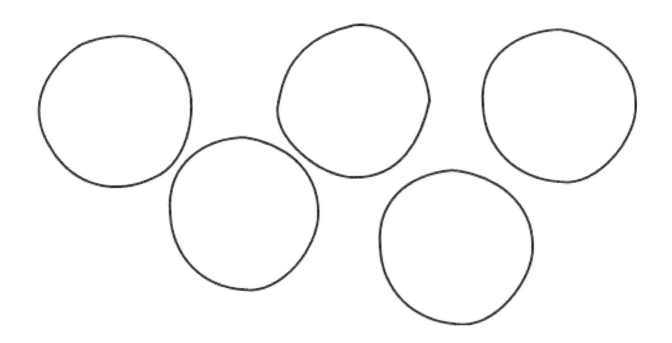

4. In the box below illustrate how your dependability can affect your students.

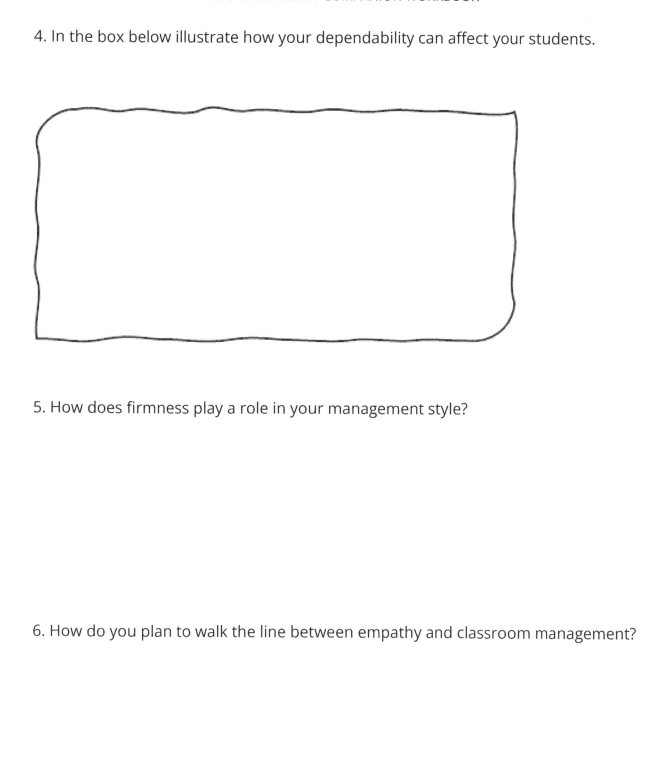

5. How does firmness play a role in your management style?

6. How do you plan to walk the line between empathy and classroom management?

7. Motivating is hard to do. What are some examples of how you were motivated as a student or in life?

8. How do you plan on using motivation in your classroom? Come up with three ways that you can enhance your lesson with motivation.

1.

2.

3.

9. Create a sample timeline of course preparation.

●——➤

10. Come up with five examples of where you can find successful tools to teach.

1.

2.

3.

4.

5.

"I like to encourage people to realize that any action is a good action if it's proactive and there is positive intent behind it."

—Michael J. Fox

Chapter Three Notes:

How to be a Successful Teacher
Word Scramble

1. OTW RAKD YRIHTT _____

2. ECIGTAHN OOTLS _____

3. AHYMPET _____

4. MEIT GMNAAEENTM _____

5. ITVNMOATIO _____

6. MEANMTGNAE _____

7. TAIEPRAPRNO _____

8. IFMR _____

9. CPPITTAEIRA _____

10. SCMOONPSAI _____

11. LOMARF SAOOSLRMC _____

12. BIXELEFIL _____

13. CAREEBLETB CECUSSS _____

CHAPTER FOUR
WHO ARE YOUR STUDENTS?

Mr. Hill's Notes:

- Know who your audience is and get to know them.

- Start by talking.

- Find common ground among students.

- Use the experience in the classroom to help you.

- Yes, there are many generational distinctions... and it is okay.

- All generations have something to share and contribute.

1. Why do you need to understand who your audience is?

2. How can your communication be affected by your audience?

3. Explain Socio-economic-status.

4. How does income relate to family structure and a student's choices they make?

5. Devise three ways you can get a new group to communicate together.

1.

2.

3.

6. What are some outside class experiences that can contribute to the success of your students?

7. How can you use your students to help you with the lesson?

7. Pick two generations to compare. In section 1 write similarities between each. In section 2 write what differences there are.

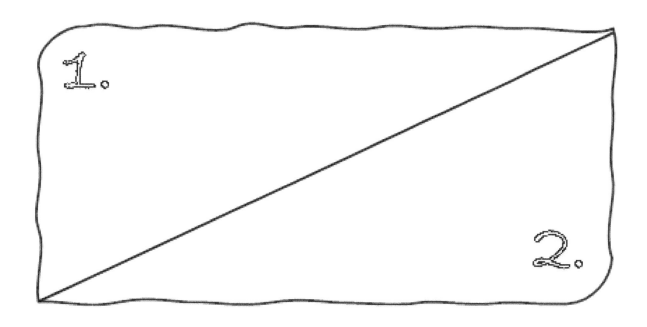

"Our chief want is someone who will inspire us to be what we know we could be."

—Ralph Waldo Emerson

Chapter Four Notes:

Who are your Students?
Dot-to-dot

1
•

2
•

19
•

•4

20
•

3
•

18
•

•5

17
•

•16

6 •

15 •

•7

12
•

9
•

14 •

13 •

8

11
•

10
•

Chapter Five
How to Educate in Emergency Services.

Mr. Hill's Notes:

- Look for teachable moments.

- Train on high-risk low-frequency events.

- Scenario training is effective education.

- Talk about the event afterward.

- Keep communication lines open and honest.

- Engage your students in the learning.

- Safety First!

- Celebrate mistakes and failures.

1. Why is scenario training better than lectures?

2. In what ways can an FTO make or break a new recruit or student?

3. Label the Dunning-Kruger Effect Chart.

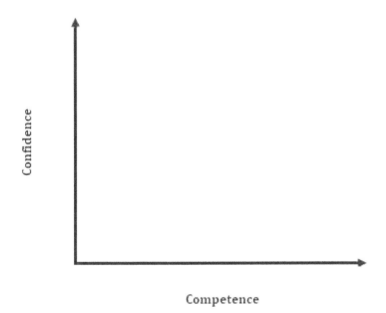

4. Within Graham's Risk Chart are Critical Core Tasks. Identify three of these tasks for an event of this nature.

1.

2.

3.

5. What is the difference between Discretionary Time (DT) and No Discretionary Time (NDT) in High Risk-Low Frequency Incidents?

6. Brainstorm your own scenario training ideas.

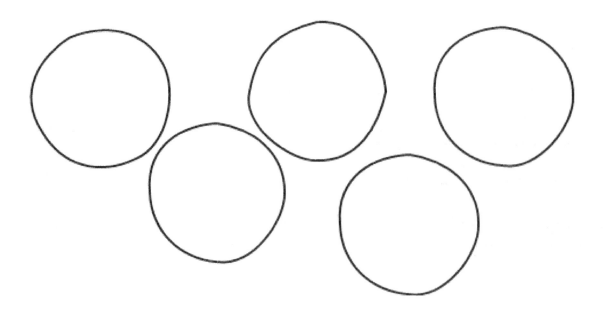

7. What role does communication play in training and how can you use it to portray real-life events?

8. Explain the difference between **QUALITY** and **QUANTITY** repetitions.

9. How does safety factor into training?

10. Create a safety plan for a "hypothetical" training scenario event.

Training Event Name:_____ Training #_____ Date: ___ / ___ / _____

Location: _____ Operational Period: _____

Identified Hazards/Risks: _____

_____

_____

_____

_____

Hazard/Risk Mitigation Plans: _____

_____

_____

_____

_____

Emergency Contacts: _____

_____

_____

"Virtually nothing is impossible in this world if you just put your mind to it and maintain a positive attitude."

—Lou Holtz

Chapter Five Notes:

How to Educate in Emergency Services
Matching Game
Match one side with the correct partner

FTO	Safety
OTJ	Low frequency
3-year salty veteran	NFPA 1584
High risk	High-risk training
Imperative	Quality
Choking child	Dunning-Kruger Effect
Time intensive	Preceptor
Rehabilitation	KSA

Chapter Six
Why Creating a Team is Important.

Mr. Hill's Notes:

- We all want to help, which is our common calling.

- Involve other subjects or fields where you can.

- Create the TEAM attitude: Together we achieve more.

- Competition can breed teamwork.

- Develop a mentor and mentee relationship when you can.

- Find other instructors to work with together as a team.

- Camaraderie will help cement the team bond.

1. What does team spirit give you?

2. How can you create a better team atmosphere where you are now?

3. What role does competition play with teams and how can you use this in your class?

4. What is the difference between a mentor and a mentee?

5. List three roles and experiences that you would require of a mentor.

1.

2.

3.

6. What are some other departments or agencies you can include in training?

"The way a team plays as a whole determines its success. You may have the greatest
bunch of individual stars in the world,
but if they don't play together, the club won't be worth a dime."

—Babe Ruth

Chapter Six Notes:

Why Creating a Team is Important
Double Puzzle

Unscramble the words to find the hidden message

EMAT ▢▢▢▢
1

TEHRAMESPO ▢▢▢▢▢▢▢▢▢▢
2 5

TENTMLYAI ▢▢▢▢▢▢▢▢▢
7

ENTIMOTPIOC ▢▢▢▢▢▢▢▢▢▢▢
11

TSIPIR ▢▢▢▢▢▢
12

TRUTS ▢▢▢▢▢
6

CTIEIXNG ▢▢▢▢▢▢▢▢
13 3

DCREAIARMAE ▢▢▢▢▢▢▢▢▢▢
10

ENETEM ▢▢▢▢▢▢
8

TRONME ▢▢▢▢▢▢
4

FMIAYL ▢▢▢▢▢▢
9

▢▢▢▢▢▢▢▢▢   ▢ V ▢▢▢▢▢▢   ▢▢▢▢▢ V ▢▢   ▢▢▢▢
1 2 3 4 1 5 4 6   4   4 6 7 2 8 4   9 10 5 13 4   4 12   11 2 6 4

Chapter Seven
The Best Way to Communicate?

Mr. Hill's Notes:

- You can't over-communicate.

- Make a great first impression.

- Talk about what is and is not acceptable to avoid misunderstanding.

- Think about your body language, look the part, and dress for success.

- Be professional in all communication.

- It's ok to say No!

- Remember to listen and hear!

1. How can communication fail?

2. Create a diagram of the communication system.

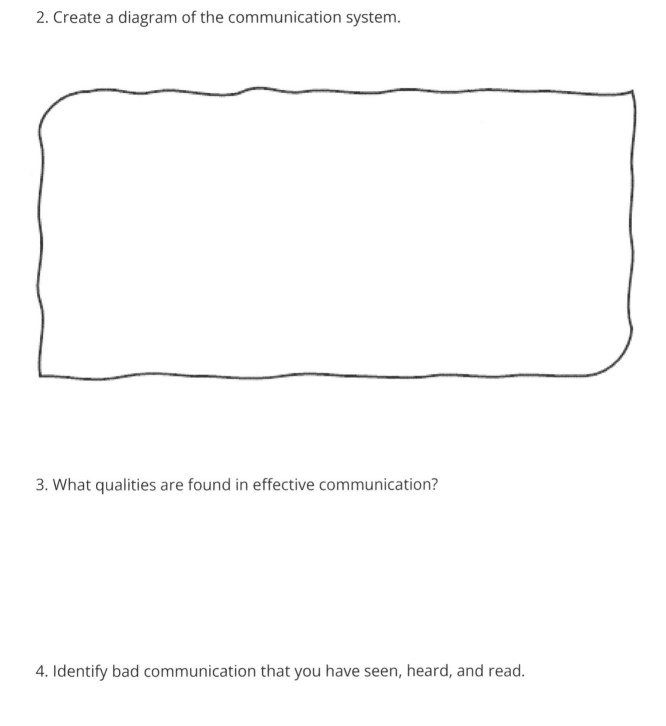

3. What qualities are found in effective communication?

4. Identify bad communication that you have seen, heard, and read.

5. Explain why your voice, tone, and feeling can affect your message.

6. Describe how body language plays a part in communication.

7. Explain new three new ways you can improve your communication.

1.

2.

3.

8. How do you plan on walking the line between sharing too much personal information and keeping a professional relationship with your students?

9. Explain why AAR and Debriefs are important learning experiences.

10. Having "the hard" talk is difficult. Describe how you would soften the blow and what strategies would you use?

"Good leaders must communicate vision clearly, creatively, and continually. However, the vision doesn't come alive until the leader models it."
—John C. Maxwell

Chapter Seven Notes:

The Best Way to Communicate
Missing Letters Game

Fill in the missing letters to solve the correct word(s)

Length of time to concentrate | A | T | | | T | | O | |

First introduction | | | P | | E | | S | I | | |

Two ears help us | L | | | T | | |

Or a misunderstanding | | I | | C | | M | | | | I | | A | | | O | |

Always professional in | | E | L | | | I | | N | | H | | | |

Accounts for more than our words | | O | D | | | | A | | | U | | | E |

CHAPTER EIGHT
WHAT YOU DO MATTERS!

Mr. Hill's Notes:

- Check your ego.

- Sweat the little things, because they can make a difference.

- Realize your importance.

- Take care of yourself.

- Patience is a virtue that saves lives.

- Be humble and honest with your students.

- Never accept poor behavior.

- Raise the bar high and strive for perfection.

1. Why do you need to check your Ego?

2. How do you want your students to remember you?

3. In what ways do the little things add up?

4. How do you plan on keeping yourself healthy and able to be at your top performance?

5. Brainstorm potential "little things" that you want to check off from a scenario training event.

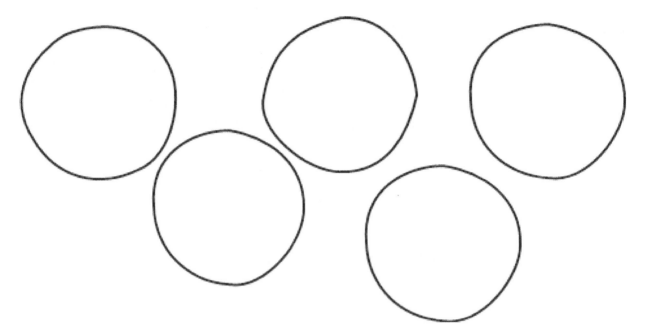

6. Explain why you need to be patient.

7. What happens when you accept poor performance?

"If you can't do the little things right, you will never do the big things right."
—William H. McRaven (Admiral ret.)

Chapter Eight Notes:

What you do Matters!
Maze

CHAPTER NINE

THE TOUGHEST CONVERSATIONS CAN BE THE MOST CRITICAL.

Mr. Hill's Notes:

- Death will be part of this job.

- Start the hard conversation with your students now.

- Give your students the tools and resources needed.

- Learn to cope with death successfully.

- You are not alone. Ask for help when you need it.

- Find positive activities to help yourself cope.

- Practice training on death.

1. What is your "bucket"?

2. How do you plan on sharing with your students effective strategies to take water out of that bucket?

3. What role does PTSD play in emergency services?

4. What is the difference between micro-stresses and emotional fatigue?

5. Why is death difficult to talk about?

6. What are some effective strategies to teach about death?

7. Create a dialogue of a death talk scenario.

8. How does stress affect a person?

9. In what ways can stress be improved in your current position?

10. Why are the easy fixes not the answer to relieve stress?

11. What is the difference between guilt and shame?

12. Describe three coping mechanisms for stress that interest you and how you plan to implement them.

1.

2.

3.

"You've planned, you've trained, you've done everything you can in your power to mitigate the stress that's facing you. And then after that, there's nothing you can do. So, you have to let that one go."
—Jocko Willink (Navy SEAL ret.)

Chapter Nine Notes:

Tough Conversations
Coloring Page

CHAPTER TEN

WHERE DO WE GO FROM HERE?

Mr. Hill's Notes:

- Always try your best no matter what.

- Sometimes you need to step back and take a breath.

- You will fail sometimes. Pick yourself up, learn, and move on.

- Positive attitudes are contagious.

- You don't need to know it all.

- Be the teacher you would want to have.

- Have fun and enjoy the journey.

1. They say the road to Hell is paved with good intentions. Can you pick out three of your biggest failed attempts from your journey so far?

1.

2.

3.

2. Now list three of the biggest successes that you have faced.

1.

2.

3.

3. Hindsight is a terrific teacher moving forward. From those failures and successes describe five critical lessons you learned.

1.

2.

3.

4.

5.

4. Positive thinking can have a real effect on your attitudes and beliefs. Create at least five achievable career goals for your next five years.

1.

2.

3.

4.

5.

5. Compare and contrast a "good" teacher with a "bad" teacher.

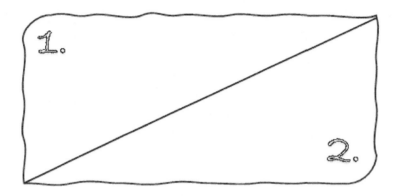

6. How can you do to improve yourself as an educational leader?

7. Create a list of resource materials that you can go back to, to help you foster knowledge and learning.

8. Explain three ways you can have fun at work.

1.

2.

3.

"The journey of a thousand miles begins with one step."
-Lao Tzu

Chapter Ten Notes:

Color your stress away!

Answers to the puzzles... I hope you enjoyed them!

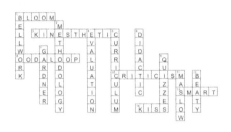

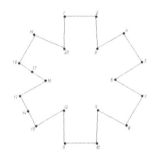

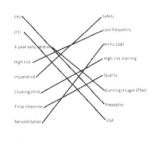

EMAT	TEAM	
TEHRAMESPO	ATMOSPHERE	
TENTMLYAI	MENTALITY	
ENTIMOTPIOC	COMPETITION	
TSIPIR	SPIRIT	
TRUTS	TRUST	
CTIEIXNG	EXCITING	
DCREAIARMAE	CAMARADERIE	
ENETEM	MENTEE	
TRONME	MENTOR	
FMIAYL	FAMILY	

TOGETHER EVERYONE ACHIEVES MORE

Length of time to concentrate	A T T E T I O N
First introduction	I M P R E S S I O N
Two ears help us	L I S T E N
Or a misunderstanding	M I S C O M M U N I C A T I O N
Always professional in	R E L A T I O N S H I P S
Accounts for more than our words	B O D Y L A N G U A G E

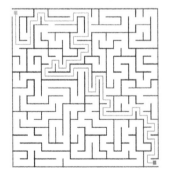

Afterword

Inspire teaching and learning in others. Being in this field is a calling and it is something that is beyond special. Not everyone can do what is asked of us. You are elite. You are brave. You are bold. And you are irreplaceable. Light the lamp of knowledge in those around you and share in the glow that is created.

Remember that learning **NEVER** stops!

Go out and be the teacher you wish you had.

"The art of teaching is the art of assisting discovery."

—Mark Van Doren

Final Thoughts:

Also By

Make sure you get the companion text for this workbook, Two Dark Thirty. When you do please leave a review for this workbook and the text.

About Author

Introducing Marc Hill, the highly acclaimed author of "Two Dark Thirty" and a seasoned firefighter/paramedic. With over 20 years of experience in both public education and emergency services, Marc is a sought-after educational consultant, speaker, instructor, and mentor. He has a distinguished career in public education, having started as a high school social studies teacher and football coach before progressing to an administrator and collegiate instructor. In parallel, Marc rose through the ranks of the fire department to become a full-time Chief, where he made significant contributions to his departments. He has received numerous personal awards and recognition, including the Core Values Award, Teacher of the Year Award three times, and many more. Marc's passion for learning and serving inspired him to become an author. Marc is happily married and has three beautiful daughters.

Made in the USA
Las Vegas, NV
25 November 2023

81482336R20044